Germany

by Julie Murray

Abdo COUNTRIES Kids

Abdo Kids Jumbo is an Imprint of Abdo Kids
abdobooks.com

abdobooks.com

Published by Abdo Kids, a division of ABDO, P.O. Box 398166, Minneapolis, Minnesota 55439.

Printed in the United States of America, North Mankato, Minnesota.

052024

092024

THIS BOOK CONTAINS
RECYCLED MATERIALS

Photo Credits: Getty Images, Shutterstock

Production Contributors: Teddy Borth, Jennie Forsberg, Grace Hansen
Design Contributors: Laura Graphenteen, Candice Keimig

Library of Congress Control Number: 2023948560

Publisher's Cataloging-in-Publication Data

Names: Murray, Julie, author.

Title: Germany / by Julie Murray

Description: Minneapolis, Minnesota : Abdo Kids, 2025 | Series: Countries | Includes online resources and index.

Identifiers: ISBN 9798384900689 (lib. bdg.) | ISBN 9798384901389 (ebook) | ISBN 9798384901730 (Read-to-me eBook)

Subjects: LCSH: Germany--Juvenile literature. | Europe--Juvenile literature. | Germany--History--Juvenile literature. | Germany--Social life and customs--Juvenile literature. | Geography--Juvenile literature. | Foreign countries --Juvenile literature.

Classification: DDC 943--dc23

Table of Contents

Germany

Germany is a country in central Europe. It is Europe's second-largest country by population. It is home to more than 83 million people.

Germany borders nine countries.

The Baltic Sea and North Sea are

on the northern border.

N
W
E
S
Denmark
Baltic Sea
North Sea
Netherlands
Germany
Poland
Belgium
Luxembourg
Czechia
Austria
France
Switzerland

Germany has coasts, valleys, and mountains. The Bavarian Alps are in southern Germany. The Zugspitze is the highest point. It stands 9,718 feet (2,962 m) high.

Germany
Bavarian Alps
Zugspitze

History

Germany was greatly affected by World War I (1914-18) and World War II (1939-45). Many Germans were left homeless from the **destruction** of war.

Munich, Germany 1945
Germany
Munich

Germany was divided after Word War II. The Berlin Wall was built to separate east and west Berlin. The Wall was torn down in 1989. The country was finally reunited in 1990.

"PEACE
ON
EARTH"

Major Cities

Berlin is Germany's capital and largest city. It is the center of business and arts. Rivers and canals run through the city.

Berlin
Germany

Hamburg is Germany's second-largest city. It is known for its art museums, lovely neighborhoods, and beautiful buildings. It is also the nation's largest **port**.

Hamburg
Germany

Food

German food is **hearty**. It often consists of bread, meat, and potatoes. A traditional dish is bratwurst and **sauerkraut**.

Festivals

Germany is known for its festivals. Octoberfest is the country's largest and most famous festival. It takes place in Munich. Millions of people join the celebration each year!

Awesome Landmarks

Black Forest
Baden-Württemberg, Germany

Brandenburg Gate
Berlin, Germany

Cologne Cathedral
Cologne, Germany

Neuschwanstein Castle
Schwangau, Germany

Glossary

destruction – the state of being completely ruined or destroyed.

hearty – large and filling.

port – a place where ships load and unload, and its nearby town or city.

sauerkraut – shredded cabbage that has been salted and allowed to ferment in its own juices.

Index